CONTENTS

CONTENTS

The Top
10
Distinctions Between
Relationship
and Religion

DISTINCTION TEN

Relationship is joyful.

Religion is painful.

The pain is increasing. People all over the planet are crying out: "There's *got* to be more than this!" The *more* that people are looking for is found in relationship with God. Unfortunately, the overwhelming majority of people are looking for more in religion. Religion cannot satisfy the desire for more. Religion only adds to the pain. The cure for the pain of religion is relationship with God.

Having a religion about God is the cause of many problems. Having a relationship with God is the solution to problems. The proof that people have a religion and not a relationship with God is the very cry of their hearts.

As long as you have a religion about God instead of a relationship with God, your cry will always be: "There's got to be more than this!"

In contrast, the cry of a person who is in relationship with God is: "Thank You! I love

You!" It is a cry of praise and worship. It is a shout of JOY!

In Scriptures it says: "In His presence is fullness of Joy . . . The joy of the Lord is our strength . . . Joy unspeakable and

Religion cannot satisfy the desire for more.

full of Glory . . . That My joy may be in you and that your Joy may be full . . . The kingdom of God is Righteousness, Peace and Joy . . ."

The Bible is full of examples of Joy being the result of relationship with God. If you are not experiencing joy on a consistent basis then chances are you have a religion and not a relationship with God.

The joy that comes from relationship is similar to the joy I experience when I look at a sunset or watch a wave break on the beach or feel a cool breeze on a hot day. I sense it when I hear my children laughing. I feel it when I laugh. Joy is the secret of an overcoming life. Sure, we all go through trials, but with joy we have power to overcome. Without joy we are weak and defeated.

> Joy that comes from relationship with God is deeper and more powerful than temporary happiness.

Joy that comes from relationship with God is deeper and more powerful than temporary happiness. Joy is internal and only depends on God's presence. Happiness is external and depends on circumstances being positive.

People in relationship with God can go through negative circumstances and still experience the Joy of salvation. For example, when the house is dirty, the kids are whining, and you are exhausted, there is still a deep peace and joy that flows from being in relationship with God. Or, when sales are down, the bills are mounting, and creditors are calling, there is still an inner assurance that God will provide. That inner assurance is the joy and strength I am speaking of. In a relationship with God there is a peace and joy that surpasses understanding. Without a relationship with God there is stress, anger, and frustration.

People in religion only feel good when things are going their way, which is not very often if you haven't noticed. Very seldom do things go the way you think they should. God's ways are higher than yours and if you really want God to do exceed-ingly abundantly above what you can ask or

> People in religion only feel good when things are going their way . . .

think then you must let go of your religious ideas of who God is and how He works.

Religion claims that it knows God and His ways but if that were true then joy would be the proof. Instead there is this deep, painful crying out for more. Religion demands that things go according to its understanding. Relationship demands that you don't lean on your understanding but instead trust God with all of your heart.

> The joy of relationship comes from trust.

People in religion are always trying to figure everything out. The problem with this is that it is impossible to figure everything out. And, trying to figure everything out will keep you from experiencing the joy of relationship.

The joy of relationship comes from trust. In

fact, there can be no relationship without trust. Of course, God is constantly working on your understanding so that you can know His will, but when things happen that you didn't foresee, it is time to let go and trust that God is in control.

I am so thankful that I don't have to figure everything out. Boy, would I be in trouble if I did. I believe that is why so many people are in trouble, because they believe they have to figure everything out for themselves. God reveals to me what I need to know when I need to know it.

The goal of this life is not to know everything but rather to be in relationship with God. And when you are, you will trust that God is guiding your life and teaching you what you need to know when you need to know it. Being in relationship means to come to a place of trusting your Creator to guide you into the purposes for which you were created. Relationship teaches with love and patience.

Aren't you thankful for God's patience? Since God is patient with you, how about being patient with yourself and trust that God is working his good pleasure in your life? When you trust, the joy starts to flow. Doubting that God is guiding you leads to depression and fear. Trusting leads to joy and freedom.

Relationship is joyful.

Religion is painful.

DISTINCTION NINE

Relationship disciplines.

Religion punishes.

Do you have a relationship with God or a religion about Him? A relationship with God always reveals a heart full of love, forgiveness, and compassion. Some of the pain caused by religion is a deep feeling of failure.

Religion sets you up to fail. Religion leads to a belief that whatever you do is never good enough. If you look deeper into the belief that whatever you do is never good enough, you will find a root of religion that says "I am not enough." The wonderful truth about having a relationship with God is that it is not about who you are or what you have done, it is about who He is and what He has done. Being in relationship requires the perception that God is love.

> Religion leads to a belief that whatever you do is never good enough.

Do you see God as a loving Father or as an angry,

impatient Deity? If your perception of God is that He is mad at you, then you have a religion about God and not a relationship with Him. Your life is a reflection of your perception of God. If you truly believe that God is loving, patient, and kind then love, patience, and kindness will flow through your life. If you believe that God is angry and impatient, then you will be angry and impatient a great deal of the time.

Relationship teaches you to see God as a loving Father. When you have a religion about God rather than a relationship with Him, you will feel like God is mad at you and that He is punishing you, again.

> Guilt and shame are sure signs that you have a religion about Jesus . . .

Countless believers battle with guilt and shame. Guilt and shame are sure signs that you have a religion about Jesus and not a relationship. A religion about Christ has no power to give you peace and often creates confusion and stress. Guilt and shame come from believing you have failed God. God understands our human condition more than you can imagine, which is why He teaches us through discipline and not punishment.

There are dramatic differences between discipline and punishment. Discipline comes from a loving Father; punishment comes from an angry, self-created version of God. Sure, God can get angry—but His anger is reserved for outright rebellion—and there is a big difference between being rebellious and being immature.

> **Relationship is about growing; religion is about failing.**

Relationship is about growing; religion is

about failing. As long as you have a desire for righteousness, peace, and joy, you are in relationship and God will show you His love through discipline. If your heart desires to do the right things, then God is not mad at you. Millions (perhaps billions) of people are trapped in a religion about God because of the lie that God is mad at them.

You must learn to stop perceiving God's discipline as His punishment. There will always be seasons in your life when God disciplines you. During those times, you must trust and have absolute faith in God's unconditional love. When you doubt God's love you move out of relationship and into religion. Doubting God's love is perhaps the greatest sin and reason why so many people struggle through life.

God is for us, not against us. He is not waiting for us to mess up so that He can punish us.

When we mess up, He is there as a loving Father to correct us and show us His way. Be thankful for His discipline. Believe in God's unconditional love for you and you will move from religion to relationship and from punishment to discipline.

It is a simple but profound truth that you cannot be a disciple without discipline. The deeper your relationship, the more disciplined you become. *Discipline* is not a popular word in our culture. It implies discomfort or even pain—although a much deeper hurt comes from the absence of discipline rather than the presence of it.

The name of the pain is *regret*. It has been said that everyone must live with one of two pains: the pain of discipline or the pain of regret. Discipline weighs ounces; regret weighs tons. Would you rather walk through life carrying around ounces or tons? The wonderful thing about discipline is that it is only uncomfortable or painful until you have established a new habit in your life. Once a positive habit is formed, the hard work ceases and the new behavior is automatic. People who consider themselves disciplined realize that short-term pain is worth the long-term benefit.

> . . . God purposefully makes us uncomfortable so that we can grow.

Why do most people avoid discipline? Because they love comfort. If comfort is at the top of your priority list, then discipline is not even on your list. People who love comfort, hate discipline. The problem with loving comfort too much is that God purposefully makes us uncomfortable so that we can grow.

Spiritual growth does not happen without discipline and some discomfort. When you are going through a tough season realize that God is disciplining you so that you will grow stronger and wiser. Understand that God is not angry with you. He is disciplining you because He loves you. Religion focuses on your sin and condemns you for it. Relationship focuses on growth and forgiveness.

Relationship disciplines.

Religion punishes.

DISTINCTION EIGHT

**Relationship is more
heart than head.**

Religion is more head than heart.

There is no such thing as a deep relationship without commitment. You make commitments with your heart and decisions with your head. Commitment is deeper and stronger than mere decision. Your heart is infinitely more powerful than your head. Your heart knows the truth whereas your head can be easily deceived. Your mind is a powerful tool but it must stay under the authority of God's wisdom in your heart.

> Your heart knows the truth whereas your head can be easily deceived.

Are you committed to following God's wisdom? What if God's wisdom is in direct opposition to what your head thinks?

Where does confusion come from? It comes from your head arguing with your heart. Many times your heart and head do not agree. Learning to follow your heart and make your head submit to God's wisdom will lead you to a deeper relationship with Him. Allowing your head to continually argue with your heart will weaken your relationship with the Lord. Your head must stay submitted to the One who lives in your heart. Are you committed to the One who lives in your heart? Have you made a commitment to seek His wisdom and be obedient when He speaks?

> Your head must stay submitted to the One who lives in your heart.

I think the reason so many "believers" fall away and don't seem to have wisdom is because they made a decision to follow Christ with their heads but their hearts never made a commitment. Your heart will stay true to a commitment even when things happen that you don't fully understand. Your head will back out of a decision when things don't make sense. The times when I have made bad decisions were when I was listening to my head and not my heart.

We have to use our heads to make decisions, but without the Wisdom of God in our hearts to influence our decisions we will make them based in fear. My heart is full of faith and my head's first inclination is to be afraid. My heart trusts and my head doubts. The reason my heart has faith and trust is because the One who I put my faith in lives in my heart.

It is your responsibility to train your head to listen to and obey the One who lives in your heart. When you are making a decision, stop and ask yourself "Am I making this decision from a place of faith or is it based in fear?" If it is based in fear then you are following your head. Decisions based in faith happen when your head is submitted to your heart. Anytime

26

your head has usurped authority from your heart you will have unnecessary problems.

Scripture declares: Trust in the Lord with all your heart and lean not on your own understanding. The head always wants to trust its past experiences and its ability to comprehend what is going on. The reason that Scripture admonishes us to "lean not on our understanding" is because our head's ability to understand is very limited.

Just because your head can't see a way does not mean that God can't reveal a way. Our heads are limited and our hearts are unlimited. The reason Scripture tells us to "trust in the Lord with all of our heart" is because our hearts are full of God's wisdom, knowledge, and understanding. Religion is so weak and limited because if it can't wrap its intellectual understanding around something, then it rejects it.

God cannot be reduced to your intellectual understanding. He is way too big and powerful for one human brain to fully comprehend. If a person rejects things they don't understand, they will be rejecting a lot of who God is and what He is doing. If you live life more from your head than your heart, you are sure to experience a lot of stress and confusion.

But, if you live more from your heart than your head you will experience much more peace and understanding. The river of God's love flows from your heart. If you train your head to follow the flow from your heart then you will live in faith and understanding instead of fear and confusion.

Scripture also tells us to be transformed by the renewing of our mind. Being transformed by the renewing of your mind means to train your mind to live by faith instead of fear.

Renewing your mind means to teach it to follow your heart. Renewing your mind means to think thoughts of faith, hope, and love instead of fear, doubt, and anger. Renewing your mind means to consciously choose your thoughts instead of allowing them to react. You can become more creative than reactive by learning to live more from your heart than your head. Your heart is infinitely more powerful than your head. Our minds are powerful tools but they are limited. Our full potential resides in listening to God's wisdom in our heart. Are you committed to teaching your head to submit to God's wisdom in your heart?

> Our full potential resides in listening to God's wisdom in our heart.

Renewing your mind is a lifelong process. Your mind is renewed by meditating on truth.

Your mind is renewed by walking in wisdom and knowledge. Beware of only gaining knowledge about God for that is the goal of religion. Relationship is a combination of knowledge and wisdom. Wisdom is the application of knowledge. Scripture declares that knowledge puffs up but love edifies. Knowledge without wisdom creates arrogance; knowledge plus wisdom creates humility, understanding, and love. Religion is intellectual; relationship is experiential. Religion is an intellectual knowledge about God. Relationship is an experiential knowledge of God's presence, which includes His grace, mercy, and unconditional love.

We are admonished to love the Lord our God with all our heart, soul, mind, and strength. If our love flows from our heart first then our mind will be renewed and we will love Him instead of our own knowledge about Him.

If our love is based in head knowledge more than heartfelt experience then we become arrogant. Some people love their theology about God more than they love God Himself. Loving your intellectual knowledge of who you think God is, is the very core of religion. The heart of relationship loves His presence.

Relationship is more heart than head.

Religion is more head than heart.

DISTINCTION SEVEN

Relationship embraces diversity.

Religion demands conformity.

A simple definition of embracing diversity is to unconditionally love people who are different than you. Do you? If you have a relationship with God, you do. If you don't, then you have religion.

Religion loves for people to be the same. In fact, it demands conformity and if you don't conform then you are either condemned, banished, or even killed. It is easy to see this truth when looking at religious extremists. Even while I am writing this book there are certain groups of people who are killing other groups of people because they believe differently. There are even religions that actively banish or excommunicate their followers for not conforming. And there are hundreds of religions, even many sects of Christianity, that condemn others to hell for not believing like they do.

People in relationship with God leave the

judging up to God. Religious people feel it is their responsibility to judge and condemn. I have personally had to repent for that attitude before God. There was a time when I was in my early twenties that I thought anyone who didn't believe like me was going to hell. How foolish I was! How religious I was! As I have grown in my personal relationship with God I now realize that it is not always a matter of right or wrong, sometimes it is just different. It is religion that preaches everyone should worship the same way.

> People in relationship understand that there are different styles of worship.

People in relationship understand that there are different styles of worship. Just because someone doesn't see something the same way as you or worship with the same style as you doesn't

35

mean they are wrong. Religion is about being right. It loves to try and prove someone wrong. Relationship is about being righteous. Part of being righteous is to embrace diversity. Part of being religious is to attack people who see things differently than you. How many wars have been started by religious people? People who are at war with God are usually at war with themselves and other people as well.

> . . . if you are having problems in your relationships with people look at your relationship with God.

Our relationships with people are a very good barometer of our relationship with God. Fighting with people is just an outward manifestation of what is going on inside. When you are fighting with God it will show up in your relationships with people. So, if you are having problems in your relationships with people look at your relationship with God and see if there is something that needs to be corrected. Being in relationship with God means you are at peace with Him, yourself, and others. If you do not have peace then you have a religion not a relationship.

People who walk with God walk with peace. Think of Mother Teresa. She is a great example of someone in relationship with God. She was once asked if she would march against a war and she said, "No, but when you have a march for peace, I'll be there." Are you standing against something or for something? This may seem like a small distinction but it is profound. Standing for is positive, standing against is negative. For example, if you are antiabortion, become pro-life. If you are antiwar, become pro-peace. If you are against premarital sex, become for abstinence. If you are against pornography, become for purity. Religion stands against and relationship stands for. Standing for someone or something is part of embracing diversity.

Religion tries to change people through negative force; relationship changes people through positive power. I said, religion tries to change people and it often does for the short-term. Relationship transforms people into entirely new creatures so they can't return to who they used to be.

Being in relationship is to be in light. Being in religion is to be in darkness. Have you ever noticed that most religious people don't know why they believe what they believe? They know what, but they don't know why. Ask a religious person why they believe what they believe and they may be able to give a lot of answers but they are all mental and there is no feeling behind it, except maybe anger because they are being challenged. Ask a person in relationship with God why they believe what they believe and they will smile and say because He is real, it is real. You can feel the positive energy flowing from someone in relationship with God. This energy is called love and love is what compels people to embrace diversity.

Anger and arrogance demand that people believe, look, and behave the same. People in religion always fight against people in relationship. Religion can't stand the freedom that people in

> Relationship empowers people to be who they are and accept others as they are.

relationship have. Relationship empowers people to be who they are and accept others as they are. God loves diversity in all of His creation, especially in people. Everyone has a different fingerprint. Everyone has a unique face. There are multiple skin and hair colors and lots of combinations. The person who embraces diversity is close to God. The person who demands conformity is far away.

Relationship embraces diversity.

Religion demands conformity.

DISTINCTION SIX

Relationship seeks to serve.

Religion seeks to be served.

Can you imagine being present when Jesus washed the feet of his disciples? The Creator of the universe humbled himself time and time again to show us the result of being in relationship with the Father. Humility is the root of relationship. It is the greatest of all virtues. Without humility there is no possibility of enjoying a relationship with God. Service is the fruit of being in relationship with God. Humility is the root and service is the fruit.

In religion, arrogance is the root and selfishness is the fruit. Scripture declares that God opposes the proud and gives grace to the humble. Many people in religion are frustrated with their spiritual experience. Little do they know, it is because of their own pride. Arrogance leads to blindness. People in relationship can see the purpose and plans that God has for them; people in religion cannot. Whatever your personal purpose is, it will be related to serving others. One thing I know for sure: purpose equals service. If someone asks you what is your purpose they could ask what is your service? My purpose is bigger than myself. God doesn't give a purpose without a service. God's plans and purposes for you are for others.

"It is not about me," is a statement that resonates deep within the hearts of people in relationship with God. Religious people think it is all about them. Religion says "here I am." Relationship says "there you are."

Do you know someone like that? I am sure you do, but more importantly, are you like that? When people see you, do they get the feeling that you are a giver or a taker? The difference between relationship and religion is where you put your emphasis. Do you seek to serve first or to be served first? We all have times when we need to serve and we have times when we need to be served. It is a false humility to think I don't need to be served. The truth is, if you are serving others then the time will come that others will be serving you. You reap what you sow. Sow service and you will reap being served.

WIIFM—What's In It For Me?

Most people are tuned into WIIFM. It is our natural radio station that we are conditioned to listen to. It is the most natural thing to think "what's in it for me?" However, relationship with God is about becoming more supernatural than natural. As someone grows in their relationship with God they tune into WIIFM less and less. They get tuned into WGWFM— What's God's Will For Me? There is peace playing on that station. There is joy playing on that station. Peace and joy are amplified when shared with others. As long as your lifestyle includes some form of service you will walk in peace and joy. When you ask what's God's will for me, the answer will include some form of service.

I once heard this saying: I dreamed that life was all joy. I awoke and found that life was all service. I served and found that service is all joy.

Service equals joy. If you think you are in relationship with God but you aren't serving others then you are deceived.

> . . . serving is an attitude more than an action.

Ask yourself: Who am I serving? What am I serving?

And always remember that serving is an attitude more than an action. People can serve with a bad attitude, but I believe that service with a bad attitude is really not service at all. A heart that truly wants to bless others is happy to serve. When you are on purpose the result is joy, not frustration. If you think you are serving God and your result is frustration then you are probably serving religion, not God. Religion seeks to be served. Remember, seek and you will find. Religion has found millions of people to serve. Religion uses people. Frustration is often the result of being used by religion. Religion uses guilt and shame to manipulate people into serving. Of course people will get frustrated when they are manipulated. This frustration is part of the pain described in distinction ten. Serving religion is painful, serving God is joyful.

Serving religion is painful, serving God is joyful.

The way you think about service determines what you experience while serving. Religion influences people to think they have to serve. Relationship influences people to think and feel like they get to serve. *Have to* versus *get to* is the difference between joy and pain. Being in relationship with God shifts your thinking from have to, to get to. The attitude "I get to serve" comes from a heart that is in relationship with God. The attitude "I have to serve" comes from a mind trapped in religion. Your mind thinks "what can I get?" Your heart thinks "what can I give?" Your mind thinks "I have to serve so I can get God's approval." Your heart knows it already has God's approval and wants to be a blessing. Remember Jesus' words: whoever desires to be great among you must become the servant of all.

Relationship seeks to serve.

Religion seeks to be served.

DISTINCTION FIVE

Relationship is forgiving.

Religion is condemning.

You have probably heard the Scripture "judge not that you be not judged." I heard it many times while growing up. I believe that verse is better translated to "condemn not that you be not condemned" because just a few chapters after that verse Jesus says, "Do not judge according to appearance but judge with righteous judgment."

Thus, it appears that Jesus says don't judge and then says judge. In the original Greek, the same word is used for *judge* and *condemn*. The truth is, we must learn to judge and we must not condemn. We must learn to judge without condemning.

One of the nastiest things about religion is that it vomits condemnation on people. One of the most beautiful things about relationship is the flow of forgiveness. People in relationship with God forgive freely and quickly. Religious people have a very hard time forgiving. They usually try to make the person feel guilty and ashamed of what they did or didn't do.

What is forgiveness? It is simply a choice to let go of an offense. Religious people get offended so easily and hold onto things for so long. People in relationship let go of offenses because they have received God's forgiveness. You can't give what you don't have. Religious people don't freely receive God's forgiveness, they try to work off their sins and earn God's forgiveness. Paying penance or working off your sin to get God's approval is a trap of religion. It is impossible to earn God's forgiveness by doing something for it. Forgiveness can only be received, it can't be earned.

Millions of people live in condemnation because they are trying to earn their forgiveness. What a hard way to live life! Relationship says,

"I forgive you because I love you." Religion says, "I might forgive you if you feel really bad and prove to me how sorry you are." Here's a clue: if you feel bad much of the time then you are in religion. Being in relationship with God feels good, real good! His forgiveness flows and flows and flows. The Lord is good and His mercy endures forever! How simple it is to just receive. How complicated it is to try and earn forgiveness.

Relationship is simple; religion is complicated. Working for your forgiveness is difficult, hard, or complicated because it is impossible. A great example is the parable about the rich man forgiving a man a very large debt and then the same man went out and demanded that someone who owed him a small amount pay him immediately. I believe that man didn't really receive forgiveness and was trying to get some money to give back to the rich man so he could earn the forgiveness. The scary thing is that when the rich man heard about the man's unwillingness to forgive someone else a much smaller debt, he put the man in prison until the original debt was paid. Do you think Jesus was serious when he said if you don't forgive men their trespasses, then neither will my Father forgive yours? People live with the pain of religion because they refuse to forgive. Part of the joy of relationship is forgiveness.

> People live with the pain of religion because they refuse to forgive.

A sign that you have freely received forgiveness is gratitude. When you have a grateful heart full of God's forgiveness, then it is easy to forgive others. Yes, I said it is easy to forgive others. Forgiveness is the natural flow from a life in relationship with God. Forgiveness is only hard when you are in religion. People in religion try to forgive because they believe they have to. People in relationship forgive because they feel the forgiveness that God has given them and they let that same forgiveness flow to others.

The condemnation that people in religion feel has two parts. One is self-condemnation and the other is condemnation from others. If you condemn yourself then you automatically give others the permission to condemn you. People treat you the way you treat yourself. When you are in relationship with God, you treat yourself and others the way that God treats you. Relationship focuses on how you treat others; religion focuses on how others treat you. Relationship takes responsibility; religion plays the victim. Religious people often say, "You shouldn't judge me." They don't understand or acknowledge that they are just reaping what they sowed. Forgiveness is simply a matter of respect. We all make mistakes. Forgiving people is to acknowledge this and move on.

Religion is great at making excuses for why it can't forgive. Religion says things like: you don't know what they did to me. They don't deserve forgiveness. They aren't sorry for what they did. I can't forgive them.

The truth is, none of that matters. Your pain is directly linked to your unwillingness to forgive. And your unwillingness to forgive is directly linked to your thinking that you have to earn God's forgiveness for yourself. Freely receive God's forgiveness and you will be able to forgive others. Millions of people have been deceived by religion to think that their bondage is somebody else's fault. People can be free as soon as they receive and give forgiveness.

They key to freedom is total forgiveness. Total forgiveness includes receiving it from God and giving it to yourself and to others. Countless people believe God for His forgiveness but then they don't forgive themselves. This is another trap of religion. Self-condemnation is a fruit of religion. Freedom is a fruit of relationship.

Relationship is forgiving.

Religion is condemning.

DISTINCTION FOUR

Relationship has friends.

Religion has followers.

What is the difference between a friend and a follower? A follower thinks you are something that you are not. He puts you on a pedestal and believes you are better than he is. A friend understands that everyone has difficulties. He knows that we all have strengths and weaknesses. Followers are mesmerized by a leader's strengths. Followers don't consider a leader's weaknesses and when the leader struggles or falls, the followers struggle and fall right along with him or her.

Religion is built on the model of leaders and followers. Relationship is built on the model of friendship.

Now, I am not saying that we don't need leaders—we absolutely do—but the idea of following a man or a woman instead of the Holy Spirit has lead many people astray. I have several leaders that I admire and respect, but I don't follow them. I learn from them, but ultimately I listen to God's Spirit in my heart.

The danger in following a leader is that you may end up doing his or her will instead of God's. Many leaders, especially in the Christian world, mistakenly think that what God has called them to do He has called everyone else to do. We are all on different levels in our relationship with God. It is a terrible arrogance to think that everyone is called to live exactly like you. The church system is experiencing failure in many areas because of this.

When we have friends instead of followers we allow them to make their own decisions and trust that they are hearing from God for themselves. I do believe that God speaks to us through people, but that's just one of His ways of communicating. Some denominations teach that God is finished speaking. They say He has spoken through His Word. While it is true that He has spoken through His Word, it is also true that He still speaks through His Spirit. In friendship with God we balance His speaking to us through the Word and the Spirit.

I find it humorous that the denominations that teach God doesn't speak to you tell you to ask God what size offering you should give. That is hilarious! I have been in a service where the message came across loud and clear that God doesn't speak to you—but ask Him how much money you should give and He will tell you. No wonder so many people in that denomination are confused about God's will for their lives.

I am aware that there is the other extreme— granola Christians—you know, the fruits, flakes, and nuts that are always saying God told me this and God told me that. The truth is that

God does speak to people through His word and His Spirit. It is not a question of whether God is speaking, the question is "Are you listening?"

Followers don't listen for themselves. Instead, they trust someone else to hear from God for them. If leaders allow their followers to look to them for God's direction rather than teach people to look to God for direction—well, I wouldn't want to be that leader when it is time to give an account for my words and actions. Religion breeds followers that can't hear God for themselves. Relationship listens with its h(ear)t for a personal God. The goal of relationship is friendship with God. Jesus said, "No longer do I call you servants but friends." Abraham was called the friend of God. Well, I am a friend of

> Religion breeds followers that can't hear God for themselves.

God and so are you—if you communicate with Him.

When I was growing up I was taught to pray and pray and pray. But never was I taught to meditate. I believe praying is me talking to God and meditating is listening for God to speak to me. It was when I added meditation to my quiet time that my relationship with God went to a deeper level.

> Relationship is about communication with God and people.

Friendship requires communication. Followers only have a monologue. Relationship is a dialogue; religion is a monologue. Relationship is about communication with God and people. Religion is about a person communicating with other people about God from their limited perception. Friends can and do speak into your life and followers can't speak into your life. Friends allow each other the freedom to see things differently. When someone thinks he heard God and the other friend thinks he didn't they can still remain friends and love each other. Religious followers always divide or separate when they have differences. Relationship creates unity and power.

Relationship has friends.

Religion has followers.

DISTINCTION THREE

Relationship is transformational.

Religion is transactional.

Religion puts an extreme emphasis on what you do. Relationship puts the emphasis on who you are becoming. Who are you today compared to who you were last year? Sadly, for many people, they aren't much different. Who will you be next year or five years from now? When you are in relationship with God, the result is a continual growing process so that you are not the same in the future as you are right now.

Have you ever noticed that there are things in your life that are not okay for you to do today but five years ago you did them without a second thought? Or, there are things that you do today that a year or two ago wouldn't have even crossed your mind? The reason that what you do or don't do is different is because you are different.

You can be religious and do all kinds of religious service and still not have grown or changed. Some people have attended church for years yet still get angry just as easily today as they did years ago. Anger is a good emotion to monitor to see if you are changing. If you have been going to church for years and still get angry easily then chances are you are religious but you don't have a relationship with God. It is impossible to be in relationship with God and not become more loving. Love is patient and is not easily angered. If you are impatient and easily angered then you are either very young in your spiritual life or you are very religious. Patience, kindness, and forgiveness are some of the results from being in relationship with God.

Remember the Oil of joy for mourning and the Garment of praise for the spirit of heaviness. These are examples of transformation. Metamorphosis is always the result of relationship. Stagnation is usually a result of religion. Religion goes around the same old mountain again and again and again. Relationship learns, grows, and goes into higher levels of life. Are you changing? It is a simple question that needs to be asked on a consistent basis. If you look back over the last few years of your life and you don't see any growth then it is time to get out of religion and into relationship.

People in relationship with God understand who they are and can see where they are going. People in religion are confused about who they are and can't see where they are going because they live in the darkness of doubt. Relationship breeds hope for the future. Hope is light; doubt is darkness. Scripture declares Christ in me is the hope of glory. That is not just future glory in heaven but also glory for the here and now. Scripture also declares that we are beholding as in a mirror the glory of the Lord and we are changed, or transformed, into the same image from glory to glory. You become what you behold. Behold His glory and you become who He created you to be. *Glory* can be a very religious, churchy word so let's give it a simple definition: *glory* is God's presence which you experience when fulfilling your purposes in life. God has a plan for who you are becoming and what you are to do.

One of the most quoted Scriptures in the Bible is Jeremiah 29:11: For I know the plans I have for you says the Lord, plans for good and not for evil, to give you a future and a hope.

Hope fuels transformation. Without hope, you stay the same; with it you are transformed. God's plan for each of us is total transformation. In relationship, you move from natural to supernatural in your thoughts, words, and actions. Be transformed by the renewing of your mind. Part of renewing your mind is to find and focus on your purposes. When your mind is renewed by God's plans for your life, you start talking and walking differently.

Who you are right now is different than who you are becoming. The focus of relationship is total transformation over your entire lifetime. The focus of religion is what you do or don't do. If you focus on who you are becoming you will do the right things and grow. If you focus on what you are doing and not doing you will stay the same. Growth is the goal of relationship. Religion keeps you the same or makes you worse.

Growth is the goal of relationship.

I once heard a line from a movie that changed my life. The movie was *1492*. In the movie, Christopher Columbus is sitting on the seashore with his son and they are watching a ship sail out to sea. After a moment, Christopher tells his son to watch as the ship disappears below the horizon. He asks his son why the ship disappeared from sight. The little boy says he doesn't know why. Then Christopher holds up a ball and says it is because the world is round not flat. And then comes the line that changed my life. Christopher says, "He who is enlightened before others is condemned to pursue that light in spite of others."

If God has enlightened you to grow in every area of life and you don't go for it, then you will live in self-condemnation because you know there is a higher calling and you are not going for it. God's purposes and plans for your life are like light.

When you know them you have been

enlightened and you must pursue them—in spite of what others think or say.

What purposes and plans has God revealed to you? When you move toward them, transformation will occur. They are revealed to you when you are in relationship with God. They are hidden from you when you walk in religious arrogance. Relationship empowers you to move from darkness to light, from fear to faith, from stress to peace, from weakness to power. Remember the Scripture "Let the weak say I am strong, let the poor say I am rich. As a man thinks so is he." The power of life and death is in the tongue. Think about, talk about, and take action with God's purposes and plans for your life and you will be transformed.

Relationship is transformational.

Religion is transactional.

DISTINCTION TWO

Relationship is freedom.

Religion is a prison.

You will know the truth and the truth will set you free. When you believe lies, the lies put you into prison. Religion is a prison. Religion feeds people lies in each area of life. The prison of religion has several cell blocks. There is the emotional cell block, the mental cell block, the physical cell block, and the financial cell block. There is divorce, depression, disease, and debt in the prison. Why do Christians have the same divorce rate as non-Christians? Why do Christians battle depression like non-Christians? Why do Christians die of diseases at the same rate as the rest of the world? Why are Christians just as deeply in debt as everyone else? Don't you think that Christians should have much better statistics than the rest of the world? The truth is, they don't. Why is that? Because most Christians believe lies in each area of life instead of the truth.

Think about freedom in every area of life. Spiritual, emotional, mental, physical, and financial freedom are all the result of walking in truth. In the Wisdom Creates Freedom Workshop I teach, if you know the truth about money, the truth about money will set you free financially. The number one reason people are in financial bondage is because they believe lies about money.

Let's look at the truth as it relates to other areas of life. If you know the truth about marriage, you will be free to enjoy your relationship. If you know the truth about how your mind works, you will be free of depression and have more peace and a lot less stress. If you know the truth about physical health, you will be free of disease.

When I say "know the truth" I am talking about an experiential knowledge, not an intellectual knowledge. People can know a great deal intellectually and still be in prison.

When you walk in the truth and take action with the truth, you will experience freedom. Wisdom is the application of truth. Applying the truth in each area of life creates freedom in each area. Now, what I am about to write is one of the most important points in this entire book: *Truth is not a doctrine or a theology. Truth is a person whose name is the Holy Spirit.* Jesus said that the Spirit of truth would lead and guide you into all truth. I believe that is a lifelong process and possibly an eternal process. It is in being in a relationship with the Spirit of Truth that you become free over a period of time. As you renew your mind with truth and take action with the truth, you are set free.

Proverbs speaks of the Spirit of Wisdom. Whether you use the name the Spirit of Truth, the Spirit of Wisdom, the Holy Spirit, or the Spirit of Jesus, you are talking about our Creator. Being in relationship with God leads to freedom. Gaining more and more intellectual knowledge about God and not getting into a relationship with Him leads to more bondage and pain.

Scripture refers to people who are continually increasing their learning but never come to the knowledge of the truth. Coming to the knowledge of the truth is to come into a relationship with God, the Spirit of Truth. Remember

> Freedom is the fruit of relationship with the Truth.

Jesus said, "I am the way, the truth, and the life." It is my opinion that many Christians know Jesus as the way, but very few know him personally as the Truth and that is why most people don't have a life of freedom. Freedom is the fruit of relationship with the Truth. Apply the truth on a consistent basis and you will find freedom.

Now, there are situations where you immediately believe and apply the truth and experience freedom. There are other situations where you have been believing and walking in lies for so long that you will not experience freedom immediately. Freedom will be a process in some areas of life. For some people, instant freedom will happen in moving from depression to peace or from disease to health or from separation to reconciliation in a relationship.

For others, freedom will happen over a period of time, as their minds are renewed and they learn to think and act differently than before. It is like some people are translated out of the prison of religion and others must walk out. For example, some people are instantly set free from drug addiction and others struggle with it before getting free. Some people miraculously turn their marriage into a peaceful place and others (maybe most) struggle in their relationship for years before finding peace with each other.

There is no one way that freedom may come but there is One Person who it comes through—and that is the Spirit of Truth. Truth sets you free and lies imprison you. In the Wisdom Creates Freedom Workshop, I teach a question that has the power to get you out of prison. If you are experiencing bondage in any area of life, ask the Spirit of Truth *what am I believing to be true that is not true?* Remember, ask and you will receive. Expect an answer and when it is revealed let it change your thinking and actions and then freedom will come.

It is in a relationship with the Spirit of Truth that you get free and stay free. The prison of religion gets people through deception. Deception is to believe something to be true that is not true. Religion is a master at getting people to believe lies and then to defend those lies with their very lives. I believe this is about to change on a large scale. The reason is in the first sentence of this book: the pain is increasing. People are starting to question their beliefs and be open to new ways of thinking and acting because they know there has to be more to life than what they are experiencing. Something inside each of us cries out for relationship with our Creator, and that relationship creates freedom.

Relationship is freedom.

Religion is a prison.

DISTINCTION ONE

Relationship is eternal.

Religion is temporary.

Religion influences people to believe that eternity starts after this life. Eternity is now. When Moses asked God who He was, God replied, "I am that I am." He didn't say, I was who I was or I will be who I will be, but I am. God lives in the present moment. The only place you can experience God's presence is here and now. Even when we get to heaven it will still be the present moment.

Religion looks so much into the past and future that it misses the present moment. Religious people may briefly experience God's presence on that rare occasion when they become present but most religious people are usually absent. When you are in the present moment you are experiencing eternity. You become aware of God's presence in you and around you when you focus on the present.

Maybe you've heard the saying "Yesterday is

history, tomorrow is a mystery, and today is a gift which is why it's called the present." The gift you receive when in the present moment is the presence of God. Relationship with God is always here and now. It is not there and then. Religious people focus on some future time when they will be with God whereas people in relationship know they

> When you are in the present moment you are experiencing eternity.

already are with God. The level of His presence and glory will certainly increase when we go to higher realms of life but the fact is that God is with us here and now. And, if you want to experience the fullness of joy that comes from His presence you must become present.

In John 8:29, Jesus said, "He that sent me is with me." In Ephesians 4:6, it says "One God and father of all, who is above all and through all and IN you all." In Psalms 139:7 and 8 King David it says, "Where could I go from your Spirit? Or where could I flee from Your presence? If I ascend up into heaven, You are there. If I make my bed in Sheol, behold you are there." He also cried out in Psalms 51:11 and 12, "Cast me not away from your Presence and take not thy Holy Spirit from me. Restore unto me the Joy of thy salvation and uphold me with thy free spirit."

> People who live in the present, live with the presence of God.

And let's not forget that the New Testament asks, "Don't you know that you are the temple of God and that the Spirit of God lives within you?"

People who live in the present, live with the

presence of God. When people stop regretting the past and fearing the future and enter the eternal present moment they will know, experientially, that the joy of the Lord is their strength.

The only good thing I can say about religion is that it is temporary. One day there will be no more religion. The arrogance, the closed-mindedness, the judging and condemning, the pain and the prison, they will all be gone for good. The prison of religion will be destroyed and people will be free. The prison's power is in keeping people stuck in the past or making them fear the future. When someone starts to focus on the eternal present they start walking out of the prison. As someone stays in the present more and more consistently

> The prison of religion will be destroyed and people will be free.

they become empowered by the joy of God's presence and they leave the prison entirely. When you live in the present you experience the presence of God and you are free.

So, the million-dollar question is: how do we live in the present moment? Here are a few answers: appreciation, gratitude, praise, and worship. I know of nothing that opens the door into the eternal present quicker than gratitude. Love, patience, and kindness are also doors into the present moment. When you behold the beauty of God's creation you become present. Look into the eyes of a child and you will become present. Listen to the sounds of nature. Feel the wind blowing on your skin or the warmth of the sun on your face.

> Forgiveness, choosing to trust God, and letting things go brings you into the eternal present.

Take a deep breath and focus on it. God breathed into man and he became a living soul. Let everything that has breath praise the Lord. Focusing on your breath and praising God with your voice brings your awareness to the here and now. Forgiveness, choosing to trust God, and letting things go brings you into the eternal present.

Prayer and meditation that flow from your heart bring you into the eternal now. God is eternal and so is His kingdom.

Remember, the Kingdom of God is within you. And the Kingdom of God is Righteousness, Peace, and Joy in the Holy Spirit. Of His kingdom and His glory there shall be no end. We are receiving a kingdom which cannot be shaken. These three things remain: faith, hope, and love.

Love is eternal. God's kingdom and His presence are eternal and eternity is in the present moment. Being in relationship is about experiencing God's unconditional love. When you choose to love, you enter eternity and experience God's presence—where there is fullness of joy and peace that passes understanding.

Relationship is eternal.

Religion is temporary.

AFTERWORD

The purpose of this book is to encourage those who already consider themselves believers to pursue relationship with God instead of playing the religious game, which is a losing game.

This book was not intended to be an evangelical tool, however I am aware that some people who have not made the decision to enter into a relationship with God may be reading this. If you are one of them, then my strong advice is to talk to the Lord from your heart and surrender your life to His wisdom. Do it in a way that is real and meaningful to you and start enjoying the journey of relationship.

Faith, Hope and Love,
Keith Cameron Smith

WHAT NOW?

Read this book often. I recommend reading it once a month until you feel the ten distinctions have become a part of who you are. Repetition is the primary way we train our minds to think differently. When we think differently, we act differently and achieve different results.

Share copies of this book with the important people in your life so you can discuss the distinctions and learn from one another's experiences and perspectives.

Go to www.keithcameronsmith.com and register for the Wise Distinctions email to receive continued support in developing your mindset for a positive attitude and success.

You can also join me for teleseminars and get information about upcoming Wisdom Creates Freedom workshops.

ABOUT THE AUTHOR

KEITH CAMERON SMITH is an entrepreneur and inspirational speaker who teaches his financial success principles to individuals and companies around the country. The author of *The Spiritual Millionaire*, *The Top 10 Distinctions between Millionaires and the Middle Class*, and other books, Smith lives in Ormond Beach, Florida, with his wife and two children.

Visit his website: keithcameronsmith.com

For more information, please visit:

www.keithcameronsmith.com